THE HOUSES OF THE OIREACHTAS

THE
HOUSES
OF THE
OIREACHTAS

JOHN McGOWAN SMYTH

Third revised edition

INSTITUTE OF PUBLIC ADMINISTRATION

Dublin

© Institute of Public Administration
57–61 Lansdowne Road
Dublin, Ireland

ISBN   0 902173   51   1

First edition 1961
Second edition 1964
Third edition 1973

This book has been set in 11 *on* 12 *pt Monotype Times Roman and printed in the Republic of Ireland by Iona Print Ltd., 33 Botanic Road, Dublin 9.*

AUTHOR

John McGowan Smyth, Bachelor of Commerce (N.U.I.), Barrister-at-Law (King's Inns), former Clerk of Seanad Éireann, entered the civil service in 1940 and served in the Valuation Office, the Department of Agriculture and the Office of the Revenue Commissioners before joining the staff of the Houses of the Oireachtas in 1944. He was Clerk of the Seanad from 1958 to 1973 when he was appointed Director in the European Parliament. While Clerk of the Seanad, he also discharged the duties of Examiner of Private Bills and Returning Officer for the Seanad panel elections. He holds a certificate in Government Accountancy and a Diploma in Public Administration. He has been a member of the Association of Secretaries General of Parliament since 1958 and was a member of the Executive Committee of the Association from 1968 to 1971.

CONTENTS

PREFACE TO THE SECOND EDITION 1969

ince the publication of the first edition of this book, numerous hanges have been made in the standing orders of both Houses, many f them for the purpose of bringing these orders into line with xisting practice, *e.g.* days and hours of sitting of the Dáil, admissiility of amendments in the Seanad. The relevant changes have been acluded in this reprint.

In addition, a very substantial part of the electoral law has been aodernised and codified in the Electoral Act 1963, which dealt, *ater alia*, with the franchise and registration of electors and with ominations at Dáil elections. The Act followed generally the ecommendations made in the reports of the Joint Committee on the lectoral Law.

The Joint Committee's recommendations relating to eligibility for lection have not yet been the subject of legislation but are set out *n extenso* in Appendix II. It may fairly be assumed that many of the ecommendations will become law, and Chapter 2, which represents he present position, should therefore be read in conjunction with Appendix II.

PREFACE TO THE THIRD EDITION 1973

Changes made in the statutory provisions and standing orders of ooth Houses since the publication of the second edition in 1964 have oeen included in this revised edition. The main change relates to the ransaction of financial business in the Dáil which necessitated the ewriting of a considerable part of Chapter 8.

Legislation relating to eligibility for election to the Houses has not yet been enacted and the proposals of the Joint Committee on the Electoral Law are therefore set out once more in Appendix II. An informal Committee on Reform of Dáil Procedure has recently reported and recommended extensive amendment of the standing orders of that House. While the Dáil has not as yet had an opportunity to consider the recommendations of the Committee and it is not possible to state to what extent they may be implemented, nevertheless it was considered useful to add a further Appendix to this book setting out a summary of recommendations of the Committee as contained in paragraph 60 of its Report.

INTRODUCTION

The 1937 Constitution (Article 15.1) of the Republic of Ireland states that the Oireachtas (National Parliament) shall consist of the President and two Houses: a House of Representatives to be called Dáil Éireann and a Senate to be called Seanad Éireann.

This book outlines the functions and powers of the two Houses and the procedures adopted by them in the discharge of their responsibilities. Such functions, powers and procedures derive first from the Constitution and secondly from law, and the rules and standing orders made by the Houses pursuant to the provisions of the Constitution.

In the course of the book, references are made to the constitutional position, procedures and practices of other countries, not to undermine any particular differences but to indicate that Ireland's system is one only of a number of systems in use in democratic countries.

While Ireland's parliamentary procedure might appear to be very complicated to the uninitiated, it must be remembered that it is carefully designed to ensure that the members have adequate opportunity to discuss proposals both in a general and in a detailed way and at the same time that business is transacted with reasonable expedition. The procedure is modelled on the British system and many of its detailed forms are explicable only by reference to British tradition and practice. Constitutional differences are not to any great extent reflected in procedure, which is determined more by the relationship between the legislature and the executive; this is generally the same in both countries.

Differences in procedure arise mainly from practical considerations: the congestion of business in the House of Commons necessitates elaborate time-tables, the committal of most bills to standing committees, the limitation of debates on the estimates to a certain number of supply days and the selection of amendments by the Speaker, none of which is necessary in Ireland nor, indeed, in many other countries which have adopted the British model.

Ireland, in common with many other countries, has adapted to its own needs a system which has worked successfully for a considerable number of years, retaining what proved to be useful and rejecting the unnecessary and superfluous such as certain traditional British rituals. The forms are not sacrosanct, and adequate powers are available for adaptation in the light of changing circumstances.

I

COMPOSITION OF THE HOUSES

DÁIL ÉIREANN

The Constitution (Article 16.2) provides that the Dáil shall be composed of members who represent constituencies determined by law, and that, while the number of members shall be fixed by law, from time to time the total number shall not be fixed at less than one member for each thirty thousand of the population nor at more than one member for each twenty thousand of the population.

The constituencies are revised by the Oireachtas, pursuant to the provisions of the same article, at least once every twelve years, and notice is taken of changes in the distribution of the population since the previous revision. At present there are one hundred and forty-four members and forty-two constituencies (based on the 1961 census figure of 2,880,752 population). The Constitution (Article 16.2.6°) further provides that no law shall be enacted whereby the number of members to be returned for any constituency shall be less than three.

The following table updates the information in *Representative Government in Ireland* by J. L. McCracken (Oxford University Press, London, 1958).

TABLE I. Number of members and constituencies

Electoral act	Number of con-stituencies	Constituencies returning						Total number of members
		9	8	7	5	4	3	
1923	30*	1	3	5	9	4	8	153
1935	34	—	—	3	8	8	15	138
1947	40	—	—	—	9	9	22	147
1961	38	—	—	—	9	12	17	144
1969	42	—	—	—	2	14	26	144

*Includes the two university constituencies, each of which returned three members.

SEANAD ÉIREANN

The Seanad, pursuant to Article 18 of the Constitution, is composed of sixty members of whom

13

2

TABLE II. Seanad General Elections, 1957–69, number of candidates nominated and elected from each sub-panel.

Panel	Number of seats	1957				1961				1965				1969			
		Nominating bodies sub-panel		Oireachtas sub-panel		Nominating bodies sub-panel		Oireachtas sub-panel		Nominating bodies sub-panel		Oireachtas sub-panel		Nominating bodies sub-panel		Oireachtas sub-panel	
		nominated	elected	nominated	elected	nominated	elected	nominated	elected	nominated	elected	nominated	elected	nominated	elected	nominated	elected
Cultural and Educational	5 (2 at least from each sub-panel)	14	2	6	3	13	2	6	3	13	2	5	3	14	2	6	3
Agricultural	11 (4 at least from each sub-panel)	13	4	12	7	10	4	11	7	12	4	13	7	11	4	14	7
Labour	11 (4 at least from each sub-panel)	15	4	12	7	10	4	11	7	11	4	9	7	9	4	9	7
Industrial and Commercial	9 (3 at least from each sub-panel)	13	3	9	6	16	3	9	6	12	3	10	6	15	3	8	6
Administrative	7 (3 at least from each	7	3	10	4	7	3	8	4	7	3	9	4	7	3	8	4

(i) eleven are nominated directly to the House by the Taoiseach (Head of the Government or Prime Minister)

(ii) three are elected by the National University of Ireland

(iii) three are elected by the University of Dublin

(iv) forty-three are elected from five panels of candidates containing respectively the names of persons having knowledge and practical experience of certain interests and services.

Pursuant to section 43 of the Seanad Electoral (Panel Members) Act 1947, the panels are each divided into two sub-panels, one of which (Oireachtas sub-panel) contains the name of each candidate nominated by not less than four members of the Houses of the Oireachtas; the second (Nominating Bodies sub-panel) contains the names of those candidates nominated by bodies on the register of nominating bodies.

At present the number of members elected from each panel are divided as follows (section 52 of the Seanad Electoral (Panel Members) Act 1947):

(i) five members from the cultural and educational panel (representing the national language and culture, literature, art, education, law and medicine—including surgery, dentistry, veterinary medicine and pharmaceutical chemistry), of whom two at least are elected from each sub-panel.

(ii) eleven members from the agricultural panel (representing agriculture and allied interests and fisheries), of whom four at least are elected from each sub-panel.

(iii) eleven members from the labour panel (representing labour, whether organised or unorganised), of whom four at least are elected from each sub-panel.

(iv) nine members from the industrial and commercial panel (representing industry and commerce and including banking, finance, accountancy, engineering and architecture), of whom three at least are elected from each sub-panel.

(v) seven members from the administrative panel (representing public administration and social services, including voluntary social activities), of whom three at least are elected from each sub-panel.

Table II sets out the numbers nominated and elected for each sub-panel in the four general elections since 1957.

The register of nominating bodies* contains the names of those bodies whose aims are connected with the interests and services

---

*See Appendix I for composition of present register.

15

mentioned in the Constitution in respect of the various panels. The method of compilation and annual revision of the register and provisions relating to eligibility for registration are contained in sections 8 to 20 of the Seanad Electoral (Panel Members) Act 1947, as amended by sections 3 to 6 of, and the schedule to, the Seanad Electoral (Panel Members) Act 1954.

2

ELIGIBILITY FOR ELECTION *

Every citizen without distinction of sex who has reached the age of twenty-one years, and who is not placed under disability or incapacity by the Constitution or by law, is eligible for membership of the Dáil and Seanad (Articles 16.1 and 18.2 of the Constitution).

The disability or incapacities may be divided into three categories:

(i) *Constitutional Incapacities*

Each of the following persons may not be a member of either House:

> President of Ireland (Article 12.6.1°).
> Comptroller and Auditor General (Article 33.3).
> Any judge (Article 35.3).

No person may be at the same time a member of both Houses (Article 15.14).

(ii) *Legal Disqualifications*

Section 51 (2) of the Electoral Act 1923, provides that each of the following persons is disqualified from being elected to either House and from sitting as a member:

(a)   a person who is undergoing a sentence of imprisonment with hard labour for any period exceeding six months or of penal servitude for any term imposed by a court of competent jurisdiction

(b)   an imbecile and any person of unsound mind

(c)   an undischarged bankrupt under an adjudication by a court of competent jurisdiction

(d)   a person who is, because of the law relating to corrupt practices and other offences at elections, incapacitated from being a member because he has been found guilty by a court of competent jurisdiction of some such practice or offence.

(iii) *Legal Incapacities*

Section 51 (3) of the Electoral Act 1923, declares that a person shall

*See Appendix II.

be incapable of being elected to sit as a member of either House who is:

(a) a member of the defence forces on full pay

(b) a member of any police force on full pay

(c) a person either temporarily or permanently in the civil service, unless he is by the terms of his employment expressly permitted to be a member of either House.

In addition, members of the boards of state-sponsored bodies are disqualified from being members of either House, *e.g.,* sections 19 (4) and 23 (6) of the Central Bank Act 1942; section 7 (7) of the Transport Act 1950; section 9 (1) of the Electricity (Supply) (Amendment) Act 1958.

In regard to membership of the Seanad, the candidates for each panel must satisfy the Seanad returning officer that they have knowledge and practical experience of the interests and services represented on the panel (section 36 of the Seanad Electoral (Panel Members) Act 1947). The section further provides (subsection (3)) that the returning officer shall have due regard to all decisions of the judicial referee (President of High Court or some other judge of the High Court nominated by him as set down in section 38 of the same Act) on questions referred to him under the Act, *e.g.,* a question of doubt relating to a person's eligibility for nomination because of statutory incapacity or disqualification may be referred to the judicial referee for his decision on the point of law involved, and the returning officer then decides whether the nomination is in order or not.

3

ELECTORATE

DÁIL ÉIREANN

Every citizen without distinction of sex who has reached the age of eighteen years, is not disqualified by law, and who complies with the provisions of the law relating to the election of members of the Dáil has the right under the Constitution (Article 16.1.2°) to vote at an election. Members are elected on the system of proportional representation by means of the single transferable vote (Article 16.2.5°).

Section 5 of the Electoral Act 1963, provides that a person shall be entitled to be registered as a Dáil elector in a constituency if he has reached the age of twenty-one years and was, on the qualifying date, ordinarily resident in that constituency and a citizen of Ireland. The fourth amendment of the Constitution Bill 1972 which provides for the reduction of the minimum age to eighteen, was passed at a referendum on 6 December 1972. It is the duty of the county councils and county borough corporations to compile the register of electors which is subject to adjudication by county registrars on claims for and objections to the entry of names in the register (sections 6 and 7 of the Electoral Act 1963).

No voter may exercise more than one vote, and the voting is by secret ballot (Article 16.1.4° of the Constitution). Postal voting at elections to the Dáil is confined to members of the Garda Síochána and full-time members of the Defence Forces (section 7 of the Electoral Act 1963).

SEANAD ÉIREANN

Section 44 of the Seanad Electoral (Panel Members) Act 1947, provides that the electorate for the forty-three members of the Seanad elected from panels of candidates shall consist of:

(i)   the members of the Dáil (elected at the Dáil election consequent on the dissolution of the Dáil which occasioned the Seanad general election)

(ii) the members of the Seanad

(iii) the members of every council of a county or county borough.

If a person is a member of the electorate by virtue of more than one of these qualifications his name is entered once only on the electoral roll.

The electorate for bye-elections for casual vacancies among the panel members consists only of the members of the Dáil and the members of the Seanad who at a date prior to polling day are then entitled to sit and vote in their respective Houses (section 69 of the Seanad Electoral (Panel Members) Act 1947).

Section 7 of the Seanad Electoral (University Members) Act 1937, provides that the electorate for the six members of the Seanad elected from the universities shall consist of:

in the case of the National University of Ireland—

every Irish citizen who has received a degree (other than an honorary degree) in the university and has reached the age of twenty-one years,

and in the case of the University of Dublin—

every Irish citizen who has received a degree (other than an honorary degree) in the university or has obtained a foundation scholarship in the university or, if a woman, has obtained a non-foundation scholarship, and (in any case) has attained the age of twenty-one years.

Every election is held on the system of proportional representation by means of the single transferable vote and by secret postal ballot (Article 18.5 of the Constitution). There is a separate election for each panel and for each of the universities.

4

NOMINATION OF CANDIDATES

DÁIL ÉIREANN

A person may nominate himself as a candidate for election to the Dáil or may, with his consent, be nominated by another person who is registered as a Dáil elector in the constituency for which he proposes to nominate the candidate (section 21 of the Electoral Act 1963).

The Electoral Act 1963, provides for the establishment and maintenance of a formal register of political parties. The registrar is the Clerk of the Dáil. A candidate is permitted to include in his nomination paper the name of the registered political party he represents or, if he does not represent a party, to describe himself as 'non-party'. The particulars will then appear on the ballot papers at an election (sections 13, 16, 21 and Second Schedule).

SEANAD ÉIREANN

At an election for panel members a candidate may be nominated either by

(i) four members of the Houses of the Oireachtas (section 25 of the Seanad Electoral (Panel Members) Act 1947), or by

(ii) a registered nominating body (section 26 of the Seanad Electoral (Panel Members) Act 1947).

The names of the candidates nominated by members of the Houses to a panel eventually comprise the Oireachtas sub-panel of the panel; lists of the nominations by the nominating bodies to the panel ultimately comprise the nominating bodies sub-panel.

A member of either House may not join in the nomination of more than one person. Registered nominating bodies for a particular panel are entitled to propose for nomination the number of persons provided for by section 26 of the Seanad Electoral (Panel Members) Act 1947, as amended by the Act of 1954.

At bye-elections for casual vacancies among the panel members, a candidate may be nominated either by

(i) nine members of the Houses of the Oireachtas (section 67 of the Seanad Electoral (Panel Members) Act 1947), or by

(ii) a registered nominating body (section 59 of the Seanad Electoral (Panel Members) Act 1947, as amended by the Act of 1954).

The choice of nominator is determined by whether the vacancy has occurred among senators elected from the Oireachtas sub-panel, or from the nominating bodies sub-panel of the particular panel.

At an election (including a bye-election) for university members, candidates are nominated in writing by two registered electors of the university as proposer and seconder respectively, and by eight other registered electors who assent to the nomination (section 16 of the Seanad Electoral (University Members) Act 1937).

5

DURATION, DISSOLUTION AND MEMBERSHIP OF THE HOUSES

DÁIL ÉIREANN

Article 16.5 of the Constitution provides that the same Dáil Éireann shall not continue for a longer period than seven years from the date of its first meeting and that a shorter period may be fixed by law. A maximum period of five years has been fixed by section 10 of the Electoral Act 1963.

Article 13.2.1° of the Constitution provides that Dáil Éireann shall be summoned and dissolved by the President on the advice of the Taoiseach. Article 13.2.2° provides that the President may, in his absolute discretion, refuse to dissolve the Dáil on the advice of a Taoiseach who has ceased to retain the support of a majority in the Dáil. To date, this discretionary power has not been invoked by a President.

The proclamation issued by the President pursuant to the provisions of Article 13.2 sets out, *inter alia,* the date of dissolution of the outgoing Dáil and the date on which the new Dáil will meet. The Constitution (Article 16.3.2°) provides that a general election for membership of the Dáil shall take place not later than thirty days after a dissolution and (Article 16.4.2°) that the newly-elected Dáil shall meet within thirty days from the polling date. The date of the poll is appointed by order of the Minister for Local Government, pursuant to section 24 of the Electoral Act 1963.

Section 12 of the Electoral Act 1963 provides that, immediately upon the issue of the Presidential proclamation dissolving the Dáil, the Clerk of the Dáil shall issue his writ, in the form set out in Part I of the Second Schedule to the Electoral Act 1963, to the returning officer (sheriff or county registrar—see section 11 of the Electoral Act 1963) in each constituency, directing him to cause an election to be held of the full number of members of the Dáil to serve for his constituency. The constituencies and the number of members to be returned for each constituency at the next Dáil election are set out in the Schedule to the Electoral (Amendment) Act 1969.

Pursuant to Article 16.6 of the Constitution, provision is made by section 14 of the Electoral Act 1963, to enable the outgoing Ceann Comhairle (Speaker), if he so desires, to be deemed to be elected to the new Dáil for the constituency for which he was a member immediately before the dissolution.

The rules for the conduct of elections to the Dáil are set out in detail in the Third, Fourth and Fifth Schedules to the Electoral Act 1923, as amended by the Electoral Act 1963.

When the count is completed, the returning officer endorses on the writ the names of the members returned for the constituency, and forwards it to the Clerk of the Dáil (section 12 of the Electoral Act 1963). A newly-elected member is notified by the Clerk to attend and sign the roll of members provided for in the standing orders. The Clerk, at the first meeting of the House subsequent to the election, makes a report pursuant to standing orders, about the issue of writs for the election and announces to the House the names and constituencies of all the members returned to serve in it.

In the case of a bye-election, the Dáil, in accordance with standing orders, passes a resolution directing the Ceann Comhairle to direct the Clerk to issue his writ for election of a member to fill the vacancy. Otherwise the procedure is analogous to that for a general election.

An elected candidate is a member of the Dáil from the date of his election to the date on which the Dáil is dissolved. On signing the roll of members, he becomes entitled to take his seat. A member of the Dáil ceases to be a member if he dies, resigns or is disqualified before the dissolution of the Dáil.

Pursuant to Article 28.11.2° of the Constitution, the members of the government in office at the date of the dissolution of the Dáil shall continue to hold office until their successors shall have been appointed.

Attendance at Dáil debates is not compulsory and no official record is kept of the members attending. If a member is suspended from the Dáil for disregarding the authority of the Chair, his suspension on the first occasion continues until the fourth day, on the second occasion until the eighth day, and on the third or any subsequent occasion until the twelfth day on which the Dáil shall sit after the day on which he was suspended. The order for suspension may be discharged by the House on receipt of a written and approved expression of regret from the member. Suspension of a member from the House does not exempt him from serving on a select or special committee to which he may previously have been appointed. As from 1 July 1973, members are paid £3,416 per annum, subject to income tax (section 4 of the Oireachtas (Allowances to Members) and Ministerial and Parliamentary Offices (Amendment) Act 1973). Each member of the House is granted travelling, postal and telephone facilities in connexion with his duties as a public representative. Travelling facilities mean (*a*) free first-class railway travel, (*b*) the repayment of fares paid on public transport, (*c*) the repayment of travelling expenses in the member's own motor car at sanctioned mileage rates, and (*d*) the repayment of any other moderate travelling expenses that are incurred. The travelling facilities granted generally include travelling between the member's constituency and Dublin, or, if the member does not reside in his constituency, between his place of residence and Dublin, between his place of residence and his constituency, and between Dublin and his constituency (Oireachtas (Allowances to Members) Acts 1938, 1947 and 1962). A subsistence allowance of £4 per night is payable to a member who makes an overnight stay in accordance with the provisions of the Oireachtas (Allowances to Members) Act 1962.

Salaries payable for ministerial and parliamentary offices pursuant to the Act of 1973 referred to above are as follows: Taoiseach £6,959 a year; other members of the government £4,430 a year; parliamentary secretaries £2,851 a year; Chairman of Dáil Éireann £4,430 a year; Deputy Chairman of Dáil Éireann £1,898 a year. In each case, the amounts are additional to the allowance paid to the member as a deputy. Pursuant to section 8 of the 1973 Act, an Attorney General who is not a member of the Oireachtas is paid £7,213; if he is a member of the Dail, he is paid £4,430 in addition to his Dail allowance.

The leaders of certain parties (other than the government party) are paid allowances for expenses in accordance with a formula set out in section 9 of the 1968 Act.

(i) Where there is one qualified party and not more, there shall be paid to the leader of that party an annual sum by way of allowance for expenses of £15,000.

(ii) where there are two qualified parties and not more

   (*a*) there shall be paid to the leader of that one of the qualified parties which is of the greater numerical strength in Dáil Éireann an annual sum by way of allowance for expenses of £10,000

   and

   (*b*) there shall be paid to the leader of the other qualified party an annual sum by way of allowance for expenses of £5,000.

SEANAD ÉIREANN

Article 18.8 of the Constitution provides that a general election for the Seanad shall take place not later than ninety days after a dissolution of Dáil Éireann, and that the first meeting of the new Seanad, after the general election, shall take place on a day to be fixed by the President on the advice of the Taoiseach.

The Minister for Local Government makes orders within seven days after the dissolution of the Dáil setting out the dates and times at which the various procedures for the election of the panel members and university members of the Seanad are to take place (section 24 of the Seanad Electoral (Panel Members) Act 1947, and section 12 of the Seanad Electoral (University Members) Act 1937).

The returning officer for the election of the panel members is, by virtue of section 4 of the Seanad Electoral (Panel Members) Act 1947, the Clerk of the Seanad. The returning officer for the National University is the Vice-Chancellor, and for Dublin University the Provost (section 14 of the Seanad Electoral (University Members) Act 1937).

The rules for the conduct of the elections are set out in the schedules to the acts referred to above as amended by the Electoral Amendment Act 1973. The returning officers for the university constituencies forward certificates to the Clerk of the Seanad containing, *inter alia*, the names of the candidates elected. The names of the members nominated by the Taoiseach pursuant to Article 18.3 of the Constitution are communicated to the Clerk by the Department of the Taoiseach. The members of the new Seanad are notified by the Clerk to attend and sign the roll of members provided for in the standing orders. At the first meeting of the House subsequent to a general election, the Clerk announces, pursuant to standing orders, the names of the members who have been nominated and elected respectively.

When a vacancy occurs in the number of members of the Seanad nominated by the Taoiseach, the Chairman, pursuant to standing orders, sends a notice of the vacancy in writing to the Taoiseach. The Taoiseach then nominates a person to fill the vacancy. When a vacancy occurs among the elected members, the Clerk, by direction of the Seanad, sends a notice of the vacancy in writing to the Minister for Local Government, who makes an order similar to that made by him for a general election. The method of election and subsequent procedure is similar to that for a general election except that there is a restricted electorate for a panel vacancy. (see p. 19).

Every member of Seanad Éireann, unless he dies, resigns or becomes disqualified, continues to hold office until the day before the polling day of the Seanad general election held after his election or nomination (Article 18.9).

Attendance in the Seanad is not compulsory and no official record is kept of the members attending. If a member is suspended from the Seanad by the Chair for disregarding the authority of the Chair, his suspension on the first occasion continues for one week, on the second occasion for a fortnight and on the third or any subsequent occasion for one month. The order for suspension may be discharged by the House on receipt of a written and approved expression of regret from the member. Suspension of a member from the House does not exempt him from serving on a select or special committee to which he may previously have been appointed.

Members are paid £2,023 per annum subject to income tax (section 4 of the Oireachtas (Allowances to Members) and Ministerial and Parliamentary Offices (Amendment) Act 1973). Each member of the House is granted travelling, postal and telephone facilities, and overnight subsistence allowances in connexion with his duties as a public representative. The facilities are similar to those granted to members of the Dáil and include travelling expenses between Dublin and the member's residence. The Chairman of the Seanad receives a salary of £2,243 per annum and the Deputy Chairman £1,203 per annum (section 10 of the Act of 1973), in addition to their allowances as senators.

PRIVILEGES OF MEMBERS

Under the Constitution (Article 15.13), the members of each House are, except in case of treason, felony or breach of the peace, privileged from arrest within the precincts of either House and when going to and returning from either House; they are not amenable to any court or any authority other than the House itself.

Each House, pursuant to Article 15.10, makes its own rules and standing orders, and has powers to attach penalties for their infringement, to ensure freedom of debate, to protect its official documents and the private papers of its members, and to protect itself and its members against any person or persons interfering with, molesting or attempting to corrupt its members in the exercise of their duties.

All official reports and publications of the Oireachtas or of either House, and utterances made in either House, wherever published, are privileged (Article 15.12).

6

POWERS OF THE HOUSES: GENERAL

The Upper House (Seanad) in Ireland, does not have all the prerogatives and powers of the Lower House (Dáil) and this is the case in most unitary states. In such states, almost all Upper Houses are appointed by a complex voting system which involves election by indirect suffrage by means of a restricted electoral college. This system is partly explained by the role of these Houses. Their function is a minor one and is confined to general debates and to proposing amendments for the consideration of the lower Houses.

In most federal states, such as the USA, the Federal Republic of Germany, and Switzerland, the Upper House has a completely different role. In these countries, it represents (usually on the basis of equal representation for each constituent element irrespective of population) the federated states which comprise the federation, and is almost always elected—in most cases by direct suffage. In such states, each House may have special rights which, though not identical to those of the other chamber, put it in a position of substantial equality. In the USA, for example, the House of Representatives has the sole power of impeachment and the sole right to initiate legislation on revenue; the United States Senate has the sole right to confirm or reject Presidential appointments and to concur in treaties. However, the Dáil and Seanad have equal and/or complementary powers in regard to the following:

(i) the Chairmen of both Houses are *ex officio* members of the Council of State (Article 31.2) and, with the Chief Justice, constitute under Article 14 the Commission which performs the powers and functions of the President in his absence.

(ii) the removal from office of
  (*a*) the President (Article 12.10)
  (*b*) the Comptroller and Auditor General (Article 33.5) and
  (*c*) a judge of the Supreme Court or of the High Court (Article 35.4). (A similar power is vested in both Houses in the case of a Circuit Court judge by virtue of section 39 of the Courts of Justice Act 1924, and in the case of a justice of the

District Court by virtue of section 20 of the Courts of Justice (District Court) Act 1946).

These persons cannot be removed from office except for stated misbehaviour or incapacity and their removal requires resolutions of both Houses.

(iii) the declaration and termination of a state of emergency requires resolutions of both Houses (Article 28.3.3°).

(iv) initiation of bills, other than money bills and bills to amend the Constitution, the initiation of which is the constitutional prerogative of the Dáil (Articles 21.1 and 46.2).

(v) the continuance in force of an act for a period longer than ninety days, the time for the consideration of which as a bill was abridged, requires resolutions of both Houses. (Under Article 24 of the Constitution, the time for the consideration of a bill by the Seanad, which has been certified by the Taoiseach to be urgent and immediately necessary for the preservation of the public peace and security or because of the existence of a public emergency (domestic or international), may be abridged if the Dáil so resolves and if the President, after consultation with the Council of State, concurs. When enacted, it remains in force for ninety days after the date of its enactment unless both Houses agree to prolong the period).

(vi) annulment of statutory instruments under various statutes. (See also the section *Statutory Instruments Committee* in Chapter 10).

The Seanad has prior or exclusive powers in relation to the following:

(i) when a bill which is rejected by the Seanad or passed by it with amendments to which the Dáil does not agree (or which is neither passed nor rejected by the Seanad within ninety days from its receipt from the Dáil), a majority of the members of the Seanad and not less than one-third of the members of the Dáil may, pursuant to Article 27 of the Constitution, jointly petition the President to decline to sign the bill and promulgate it as a law because it contains a proposal of such national importance that the will of the people ought to be ascertained. If the President, after consultation with the Council of State, decides to accept the petition, the bill must be approved by the people at a referendum or by resolution of a new Dáil within eighteen months of the decision, before it may be signed and promulgated, No case has arisen under this provision.

(ii) the certificate of the Ceann Comhairle under Article 22.2 of the Constitution, that a bill is a money bill, may be challenged by a resolution of the Seanad requesting the President to refer the question to a Committee of Privileges consisting of an equal number of members of both Houses and a judge of the Supreme Court as chairman. If the President accedes to the request, the matter is determined finally and conclusively by the Committee. No case has arisen under this provision.

(iii) the President may sign a bill earlier than the fifth day after the date on which it is presented to him at the request of the government, with the prior concurrence of the Seanad (Article 25.2.2°). This occurs comparatively frequently, *e.g.* in case of bills which have to be enacted by a specified date.

(iv) initiation of private bills (pursuant to standing orders relating to private business).

The relatively superior powers of the Dáil may be appropriately considered under three headings: control over the executive, the finances of the state, and legislation. The procedure of the Houses in dealing with the three elements are outlined in some detail in the following chapters.

7

POWERS OF THE HOUSES: CONTROL OVER THE EXECUTIVE

Under the Constitution (Article 28.4.1°), the government is responsible to the Dáil alone. This responsibility pertains to the right of the Dáil to nominate the Taoiseach, to approve of the nomination by the Taoiseach of the other members of the government and, when the government is appointed by the President, to examine and criticise its administration.

(i) *Appointments of the Taoiseach and other Members of the Government.*

Article 13.1.1° of the Constitution provides that the President shall, on the nomination of the Dáil, appoint the Taoiseach. The President, on the nomination of the Taoiseach and with the prior approval of the Dáil, appoints the other members of the government (Article 13.1.2°). It is customary (though not mandatory) for the Taoiseach to inform the Dáil of the departments to which he has assigned the ministers.

All members of the government, numbering not less than seven and not more than fifteen (Article 28.1), must be members of either House (Article 28.7). The Taoiseach, Tánaiste and Minister for Finance must be members of the Dáil and not more than two of the other ministers may be members of the Seanad (Article 28.7).

From time to time the government may, on the nomination of the Taoiseach, appoint not more than seven members of the Houses of the Oireachtas to be parliamentary secretaries to the government or to executive ministers and may at any time remove any parliamentary secretary so appointed (section 7 of the Ministers and Secretaries Act 1924).

Every member of the government has the right to attend and be heard in each House (Article 28.8). Parliamentary secretaries are accorded a similar right by the standing orders of both Houses.

The government meets and acts as a collective authority and is collectively responsible for the departments of state administered by its members (Article 28.4.2°).

The Constitution (Article 28.10) provides that the Taoiseach shall resign from office if he ceases to retain the support of a majority in the Dáil, unless on his advice (which is not necessarily accepted (Article 13.2.2°)), the President dissolves the Dáil and the Taoiseach secures the support of a majority of the newly reassembled Dáil. The Taoiseach's resignation terminates the appointment of the other members of the government, but all members, including the Taoiseach, carry on their duties until their successors are appointed (Article 28.11)

It should be pointed out at this stage that the provisions relating to membership of the government, and the appointment and dismissal of governments, with which we are familiar in Ireland, are not necessarily common to all democratic countries. To take an extreme example: the executive in the United States is practically independent of both Houses of the Legislature, and members of the government are appointed by the President without any reference to the House of Representatives. However, these appointments require the consent of the Senate.

In the United Kingdom, although the government must depend on retaining the support of a majority in the House of Commons, neither the Prime Minister nor the other members of the government require to be formally nominated by the House.

Similarly, in other countries such as Australia and India, persons other than members of parliament may, at any rate initially, be appointed members of the government. In certain countries, members of parliament who are appointed ministers lose their rights in parliament (in Brazil, France and Switzerland for example) or even their seats, as in the USA. This latter requirement arises from what seems to Irish people a rather rigid application of the doctrine of the separation of the powers of the executive and the legislature.

The power of dissolution in Ireland, as in the United Kingdom, is one of the most important features that distinguish this system from that in force in the USA and in many other countries. Its absence from the US system is a logical consequence of the separation there of the executive and legislative bodies, which for specified periods continue independently of each other.

In certain countries, such as Switzerland and Brazil, the executive cannot prematurely end the term of parliament by dissolution; in others, like Austria and the Federal Republic of Germany, dissolution is limited by legal or constitutional requirements. It may be noted that Article 12 of the French Constitution of October 1958 states that the President of the Republic may, after consultation with the Premier and the Presidents of the two Houses, dissolve the

National Assembly. No further dissolution can take place within a year following the election of a new National Assembly. This is a stronger provision than the analogous one in the previous Constitution.

The power of dissolution, by or on the advice of the executive, acts as a powerful deterrent to capricious withdrawal of confidence by parliament. It has been frequently held that the absence or curtailment of such a power leads in many cases to frequent changes of government, and not always for compelling reasons.

(ii) *Control of Administration*

The Dáil has a number of exclusive constitutional responsibilities in connexion with executive action: to consider the estimates of receipts and expenditure of the state (Article 17.1), to approve international agreements involving charges upon public funds (Article 29.5.2°), and to assent to a declaration of or participation in war (Article 28.3.1°).

The most immediate control of public administration exercised by the Dáil is the parliamentary question. Members have the right to address questions to ministers about public affairs connected with their departments or on matters of administration for which the ministers are officially responsible. These questions are in writing and normally require three days notice. They are answered by the members of the government at sittings of the House on Tuesdays and Wednesdays from 3 p.m. to 4 p.m., and on Thursdays from 2.30 p.m. to 3.30 p.m. A question relating to a matter of urgent public importance may, with the permission of the Ceann Comhairle, be asked on private notice to a member of the government (see for example, *Dáil Debates*, Vol. 264, Cols. 45/9 of 28/11/72). *Ad hoc* supplementary questions may be allowed, at the discretion of the Chair.

The Chair has no power to compel a minister to answer a question. Although ministers normally have statutory authority to seek information concerning the activities of state-sponsored bodies, they generally refuse to answer questions relating to the day-to-day administration of these bodies and cannot be compelled by the Chair to do so. However, they may supply the required information; *e.g.* it is the practice to do so in the case of the Electricity Supply Board's rural electrification activities.

Members may also submit questions for written reply, and when the answers have been given they are printed in the official report. Questions cannot lead to a debate or to a vote; neither can the half-hour discussion on the adjournment which a member, who is dissatisfied with an answer, may initiate with the consent of the Chair. However, a matter to be raised on the adjournment in either House need not necessarily arise out of a question (it obviously never does in the Seanad where there is no provision for questions), nor is it automatically in order for the adjournment debate merely because it has been the subject of a question. The Chair, in the Dáil or Seanad, would not allow a matter to be raised for which a minister has no official responsibility: the Minister for Lands answers questions relating to the activities of the Land Commission, but they may not be pursued on the adjournment, since he is not officially responsible for the Commission's decisions. The Chair would also not allow discussion on a matter which involves the advocacy of legislation which is *sub judice,* or which may more properly be brought forward as a substantive motion.

However, there is another form of motion on the adjournment which may give rise to a decision: a motion, submitted by a member to the Chair at the commencement of public business, to adjourn the House on a matter of urgent public importance. In the Dáil such a motion may be made if a member, who has given notice to the Ceann Comhairle before the opening of the sitting, rises in his place at the commencement of public business and states that he requests leave to move the adjournment of the Dáil in order to discuss a matter of urgent public importance. He then states the matter. If the Ceann Comhairle considers that the motion is one contemplated by the standing order, and not less than twelve members support it, he gives leave for the motion to be moved at 9 p.m. on a Tuesday or Wednesday, at 3.30 p.m. on a Thursday, or at such hour on the day the request is made that the Dáil appoints. A matter which fails to obtain the requisite support cannot be brought forward under the standing order again for the following six months.

A similar procedure exists in the Seanad, except that prior notice is not required by the standing order (although in practice it is usually given). The number of members required to support the motion is five and the Cathaoirleach fixes the hour (on the same day) at which the motion shall be moved.

Substantive motions, even though they do not relate to matters involving ministerial responsibility and despite the fact that they advocate legislation, may be put down by members of the Dáil or Seanad, but they may not be discussed while their subject matter or matters having a bearing on them are *sub judice*. However, the standing orders of both Houses provide that no members may reopen discussion on a question decided within the previous six months and also prohibit the discussion by way of anticipatory motions of matters already appointed for consideration.

Four days notice of such motions is required. The Dáil standing orders provide that motions or bills to be moved by private members shall be taken between 6 p.m. and 7.30 p.m. on Tuesdays and Wednesdays, but a member of the government may move, without notice, at the commencement of public business on these days, that government business not be interrupted at the times specified. Time is not given to private members' business during the period when the ordinary yearly resolutions voting money for public services or imposing taxation, or when the bills implementing such resolutions are under consideration (standing order 83). The number of hours devoted to private members' motions in the years 1963–71 are set out in Table III on p. 55. It must be remembered, however, that the figures give a very incomplete picture of private members' rights, because during financial business they have an opportunity to speak on the estimates and to criticise administration; occasionally they have been allowed to discuss a motion relevant to the activities of the department or office concerned with an estimate. In recent years, government motions to approve policy decisions have occurred more frequently, thus allowing private members further opportunities for debate. Moreover, the parliamentary question is always available to deputies.

The standing orders of the Dáil provide for precedence to be given to private members' motions. A party which had not less than seven members elected at the previous general election, or all deputies who are not members of any party, constitute a group which has the right to nominate in rotation a private member of the group to move a motion in his name. The order by which the right is exercisable is determined by the number of members in the group, and larger groups have precedence over smaller ones. When there is an equal number of members, precedence is determined by lot.

The nominated member gives notice to the Ceann Comhairle of the motion he proposes to move, at least ten days prior to the date on which it is moved, and appropriate precedence is given to it in the private members' business on the Order Paper.

The time allowed for debate on a private members' motion, but not any stage of a private members' bill, is restricted to three hours in the Dáil (standing order 87). The speech of a member proposing a motion to which the time limit applies may not exceed forty minutes and he, or another member authorised by the proposer and

35

who has not already spoken, is entitled to not less than fifteen minutes in reply. The speech of any other member participating in the debate may not exceed thirty minutes.

In the Seanad, pursuant to the resolution adopted on 10 February 1971 (*Seanad Debates* Vol. 69, Cols. 581/4), one full sitting day in each month is devoted to private members' motions, unless the Seanad otherwise orders. The time allowed is restricted to six hours, unless the House otherwise orders. The speech of the member proposing the motion may not exceed thirty minutes, and he, or another senator who is so authorised by the proposer and who has not already spoken, is entitled to not more than twenty minutes in reply. The speech of any other senator taking part in the debate may not exceed twenty minutes.

8

POWERS OF THE HOUSES: FINANCES OF THE STATE

The Dáil has the superior constitutional authority in relation to the finances of the State, and the Seanad's duty concerning finance is limited to the consideration, within twenty-one days, of the bills giving legislative effect to financial proposals. For convenience, the procedure is outlined in chronological order.

The Constitution (Article 28.4.3°) states that the government shall prepare estimates of the receipts and estimates of the expenditure of the state in each financial year and shall present them to Dáil Éireann for consideration. It further provides (Article 17.1.1°) that, as soon as possible after their presentation, the Dáil shall consider the estimates. Standing Order 121 provides that the Estimates for Public Services shall be presented to the Dáil not later than the 30 April in each year.

Pursuant to the constitutional directive, two documents known as the Estimates for Public Services and the Estimates of Receipts and Expenditure are presented to Dáil Éireann each year. The former is generally presented early in March, and the latter becomes available some days before the Budget statement which is generally made early in May. The Estimates for Public Services is a substantial volume giving detailed information of the estimates of expenditure on the supply services, which require to be approved each year. The Estimates of Receipts and Expenditure show in a concise form (i) the estimates of total expenditure for the financial year, (ii) the estimates of receipts for the financial year based on the tax rates in force, and (iii) the amounts of actual receipts and expenditure for the previous financial year. The estimates of total expenditure in this document include the expenditure on the supply services, expenses on Central Fund services (i.e. those services not subject to annual vote, such as service of public debt, road fund, judicial salaries), and expenditure on capital and other issues. The Dáil is able to determine whether or not the Minister for Finance needs to procure additional moneys by taxation, borrowing or by some other means.

Estimates for Public Services

The Dáil Committee on Finance discusses these Estimates individually or in related groups; they consider motions for granting sums for the services provided by the Estimates. To enable the public services to be financed during that part of the financial year when the Estimates for them are being considered, the Central Fund (Permanent Provisions) Act 1965 authorises the Minister for Finance to issue from the Central Fund an amount not exceeding four-fifths of the amount appropriated for each particular service during the preceding financial year and to use this sum to make good the supply for such services. The Act provides that any sum so issued shall be increased or reduced depending on the size of the supply eventually granted by the Dáil for the particular service. In March of each year, the Minister for Finance lays before the Dáil a statement of the sums which the Act authorises him to issue in the following financial year.

The Committee on Finance originated in Britain at the beginning of the seventeenth century at a time when the Commons was asserting its rights in financial matters over the Crown. When the House went into committee, the Speaker was moved from the Chair and, since he was expected at that time to look after the interests of the King, the device removed his constraining presence. The debate in committee was fuller and more detailed, since members had the right to speak more than once. Although the original political reason for the practice has long since disappeared, the formula has been retained and has been adopted in many parliaments which have modelled their procedure on the British. Technically, a member of the Dáil still has the right to speak more than once in Committee on Finance; it is customary, however, to confine him to one speech. The House has, of course, a further opportunity to consider the resolutions on report.

It is observed practice that the debates on the Estimates are directed towards discussion of the preceding year's administration and of new services included in the Estimate. It is not permissible to criticise existing legislation or to advocate its amendment.

If a member wishes to challenge policy, a motion to refer back the Estimate for reconsideration is made immediately after the conclusion of the opening speech on the Estimate by the minister or parliamentary secretary concerned.

Under standing orders of the Dáil, only a member of the government may move a motion authorising expenditure (e.g. an estimate), a motion authorising a charge upon the people (a taxation motion in connexion with the Budget), or an amendment to either one necessitating an increase in the amount named in any such motion. The basic constitutional provision in regard to expenditure provides

Article 17.2) that the Dáil shall not pass any vote or resolution, and no law shall be enacted, for the appropriation of revenue or other public moneys unless the purpose of the appropriation shall have been recommended to the Dáil by a message from the government signed by the Taoiseach.

When all the Estimates have been agreed to, a bill is introduced to appropriate the total sum in the manner detailed in the schedule, and this passes through the usual stages in both Houses. In recent years the Appropriation Bill has been dealt with at the end of the calendar year. In December 1971, the Seanad passed the Bill in a formal way but postponed the debate on it until the following January, when it discussed a motion noting the supply services and purposes to which sums had been appropriated by the Appropriation Act of 1971 (*Seanad Debates*, Volume 72, Cols. 51, et seq.). The procedure was repeated in 1972/73.

If, in the course of a financial year, it is discovered that the amount provided in the estimate is not sufficient or that a new service is required, a supplementary or additional estimate may be introduced by the appropriate minister. The debate on the supplementary vote is confined to the items constituting the vote and no discussion may take place on the original vote except in so far as it may be necessary to explain or illustrate the particular items under discussion.

If, however, expenditure in excess of the Estimate is not brought to notice until the expiry of the appropriate financial year, this expenditure requires an Excess Vote. The practice is to refer such Excess Votes to the Committee of Public Accounts and, on publication of its report, the Dáil considers the Votes (see, for instance Interim Report T.209 of the Committee of Public Accounts of 8 June 1966 and *Dáil Debates*, Vol. 226, Col. 111, et seq.). The sums voted as a result of the supplementary estimate or Excess Vote are appropriated by the Appropriation Bill which is introduced after the Dáil has agreed to such estimate or vote.

Budget

The annual statement of the Minister for Finance, in which he submits his Estimates of Receipts and Expenditure for the current financial year, is made to the Dáil in April or May. In the statement, the Minister outlines, among other things, his proposals for new taxation and indicates the proposed changes to the existing tax structure. When he has concluded his statement, it is customary for a representative to make an *ex tempore* reply, on behalf of each opposition party, after which financial motions (the terms of which are not disclosed until then) embodying the taxation proposals outlined by the Minister, are submitted to the Dáil for consideration in the Committee on Finance. When the motions are passed by the Committee, they are reported to the House and are again considered by the House on report.

Generally, it is considered necessary that financial resolutions imposing new taxation or varying existing taxation should, in the interests of the revenue, be given statutory effect from the day upon which the proposals which they contain are made public. Therefore, the resolutions contain declarations that it is expedient that they should have statutory effect under the Provisional Collection o Taxes Act 1927, normally for a period not exceeding four months from the date of operation. The practice is that the resolutions are passed in committee on the day on which the Budget statement is made, the main debate on the Minister's statement being reserved for the final or general motion which is usually "That it is expedient to amend the law relating to customs and inland revenue, and to make further provisions in connexion with Finance."

The Finance Bill for the year, which is based upon the financial resolutions, is introduced by the Minister for Finance as soon as practicable after the resolutions have been agreed to by the Dáil; its enactment gives the resolutions legislative effect.

9

POWERS OF THE HOUSES: LEGISLATION

The Dáil has superior constitutional powers regarding legislation in the following instances:

(i)   a money bill, as defined in Article 22 of the Constitution, or a bill to amend the Constitution may be initiated only in that House. The Seanad has only twenty-one days to consider money bills and may make recommendations only in regard to them; it cannot amend them and can delay them for only a very limited time.

(ii)   a bill, to which the Seanad does not agree, may be deemed to be passed by both Houses, pursuant to a resolution of the Dáil to that effect, within 180 days of the expiration of the ninety days period which the Seanad has for considering the bill (Article 23.1).

Bills may be divided into two main categories: public bills and private bills.

PUBLIC BILLS

Public Bills (with the exception of Consolidation Bills) go through five stages in the House in which they are initiated.

First Stage

When a bill is to be initiated in the Dáil, its title and a short description of its purpose (the long title), prepared by the proposer and accepted by the Ceann Comhairle, appears on the Order Paper. The member giving notice moves for leave to introduce the bill. If this motion is opposed, the Ceann Comhairle, after permitting an explanatory statement from the member presenting the motion and a statement from a member who opposes the motion, puts the question thereon. If permission is given to introduce the bill, an order is made for its consideration on second reading and the bill is printed. This is usually a formal stage agreed to without debate, particularly in the case of government bills, and is tantamount to an order for printing the bill. It arises only in the initiating House, and when the bill has been passed by that House, it is first considered on second stage in the other House.

A government bill is introduced in the Dáil by a member of the government or by a parliamentary secretary.

In the Seanad, a government bill is introduced by the Leader of the House. In the case of private members' bills, the initiative is exercised by not less than three or more than six senators and the member whose name appears as first signatory on the bill moves for leave to introduce it.

It has been urged frequently that bills of an administrative or technical nature should normally be introduced in the Seanad to enable that House to proceed with its legislative business while the Dáil debates the estimates. This would obviate the situation that often arises at the end of July each year when the Seanad finds itself with a large number of bills to deal with after the Dáil has gone into recess. In recent years, several government bills have been introduced in the Seanad and this has led to a more uniform progress of legislation.

Second Stage

The debate on the motion "That the Bill be now read a second time" is confined to the general principle of the bill, since matters of detail are more appropriately dealt with at the next stage. It is permissible for members to raise matters that they feel could relevantly be included in the bill.

In the Dáil, two kinds of amendments may be made to the motion:

(i) by omitting the word "now" and adding at the end of the motion "this day three months" or some other date.

(ii) by omitting all or some of the words after "That" and substituting words stating some special reason against the second reading.

The second type of amendment is the only one that may be moved in the Seanad at this stage. If the second reading is agreed to, the bill is ordered to be considered in committee. This is usually a committee of the whole House but it may be a special or select committee. This contrasts with the practice in the British House of Commons where bills are invariably sent 'upstairs' to the standing committees. However, in the Dáil, a private member's bill which receives a second reading must be referred to a select or special committee.

Third (Committee) Stage

The bill is considered section by section in committee; amendments may be made, sections deleted and new sections inserted.

Amendments must be relevant to the subject matter of the bill and must not be in conflict with the principle of the bill as read a second time. An amendment must be directed to omitting, adding or substituting words but may not be equivalent to a direct negative (e.g. to delete a section, since the same result is obtained by voting against the question "That the section stand part of the Bill") or inconsistent with a previous decision.

An amendment necessitating state expenditure or a charge on the people must be covered by a money resolution (authorising expenditure) or a financial resolution (authorising a charge) to the bill. If such a resolution is fundamental (Appropriation Bill and the Finance Bill), it must be agreed to by the Dáil prior to the introduction of the bill but, if it is incidental, it may be taken at any time prior to the committee stage. An amendment to increase expenditure or a charge may be moved only by a member of the government.

In the Seanad, government amendments are proposed from the Chair or moved by a senator who is a member of the government.

In committee, as distinct from in the House, a motion or amendment need not be seconded and a member may speak more than once on the same question. When the sections have been disposed of, the schedules, the preamble (if any), and the long title to the bill are considered and amended, if this is necessary. The bill is then reported with or without amendment to the House and an order is made for its consideration on report. Variations in this procedure are permissible if they are authorised by instructions from the House.

A special committee deals with the bill in the same way as the committee of the whole House, whereas a select committee normally has power to send for persons, papers and records to take oral and written evidence. A bill reported from a special committee may be recommitted to a committee of the whole House or to any other committee, but a bill reported from a select committee with power to send for persons, papers and records must, under the standing orders, be recommitted to a committee of the whole House. A special committee merely reports the bill with or without amendments, whereas a select committee may report in addition its opinions and observations and any minutes of evidence given before it.

The special committee procedure is the normal way to deal with private members' bills (see p. 46) and those government bills that are not dealt with in committee on the floor of the House: Defence Bill 1951, Factories Bill 1956, Companies Bill 1962. The government bills sent to such committees have usually been those of a technical or consolidating nature. The select committee procedure is used

43

mainly in the case of private bills, since it facilitates the hearing of counsel and the examination of witnesses, (see p. 46). This procedure is mandatory under standing orders relating to private business.

Fourth (Report) Stage

At this stage, the bill as reported from the committee is considered *in toto* and amendments may be made. Amendments previously rejected in committee may not be moved, nor may amendments be moved which involve a charge upon local rates or impose pecuniary penalties, unless the House decides to recommit the bill in respect of them. In general, permissible amendments are drafting and minor amendments and those that substantially arise out of the proceedings of the committee. Debate on this stage is usually confined to any amendments which are moved. When the amendments have been disposed of, the question "That the Bill (or the Bill, as amended) be received for final consideration" is decided and an order for the fifth stage is made.

Fifth Stage

On this stage, a general debate on the contents of the bill is permissible, but only verbal amendments may be made. The question proposed on ordinary (i.e. non-money) bills in each House is "That the Bill do now pass" but, in the case of a money bill, the question proposed in the Seanad is "That the Bill be returned to the Dáil". When a bill is passed and has been sent to the other House, it is deemed to have passed its first stage in that House and is set down for its second stage. When the Seanad passes a Dáil bill with amendments, the Dáil considers these in committee. If the Dáil does not agree with all or any of the Seanad amendments, the matter is reconsidered by the Seanad which may decide whether or not to insist on the amendments. If it decides to insist, the provisions of Article 23.1.1° of the Constitution apply (see p. 41).

If the Seanad bill is amended in the Dáil, it is deemed to be a bill initiated in the Dáil (Article 20.2.2°) and is put down in the Seanad pursuant to standing orders, for its fourth stage, and considered on that and the fifth stage only.

A bill which lapses before it has reached its final stage, because of the dissolution of the Dáil, may be dealt with on the reassembly of the Dáil at the stage it had reached prior to the dissolution; a resolution of the Dáil restoring it to the Order Paper is necessary. The bill is proceeded with at the commencement of the particular stage which it had reached prior to the dissolution, unless the resolution directs otherwise. A similar procedure may be adopted by the Seanad.

When a bill, other than a bill to amend the Constitution, is passed or deemed to have been passed by both Houses, it is sent to the President for his signature and promulgation as law (Article 25.1). The President signs the bill not earlier than the fifth day and not later then the seventh day after the date on which the bill is presented to him, unless a motion requesting his earlier signature is agreed to by the Seanad (Article 25.2) (see p. 30), or unless he decides to refer the bill to the Supreme Court (Article 26) or to a referendum (Article 27) (see p. 29). A bill to amend the Constitution which is passed or deemed to have been passed by both Houses and is approved of at a referendum (Article 47) is signed forthwith by the President (Article 46.5).

CONSOLIDATION BILLS

A Consolidation Bill is a bill which is certified by the Attorney General as not containing substantive amendment of the law; it may be introduced in either House, but is invariably initiated in the Seanad. After receiving a second reading, it is referred to the Standing Joint Committee on Consolidation Bills (see Chapter 10) which reports it with or without amendment to both Houses.

The bill is then considered on the fourth and fifth stages in the initiating House and is then sent to the other House where the first, second and third stages are waived and it is considered on the fourth and fifth stages only. It is then enacted in the same way as an ordinary bill.

PRIVATE MEMBERS' BILLS

A private member's bill is a public bill introduced by a member who is not a member of the government or a parliamentary secretary.

If a motion for leave to introduce such a bill is opposed in the Dáil, the debate is adjourned until the next Tuesday or Wednesday on which private members' business is taken. Such a bill takes precedence over all private members' motions other than those on which debate has commenced. The second stage is also taken in private members' time and, if agreed to, the bill is referred to a special or select committee. Bills involving incidental expenditure or taxation cannot proceed beyond the second stage without the appropriate money or financial motion being moved by a member of the government. Bills introduced by private members can be 'killed' at that stage if they are not approved of by the government. Only very rarely, however, will they proceed even so far. The final stages are also taken in private members' time.

In the Seanad, a private member's bill proceeds in the same way as a government bill. The only limitation in the standing orders is that government bills take precedence over those of private members.

From 1965 to 1969, eleven bills were brought forward in the Dáil by private members. The motion for leave to introduce one was withdrawn, and five were negatived on the first stage; one was withdrawn and four rejected. The chances of a private member's bill reaching the statute book are remote, for even when the government accepts the principle of the bill, the member is normally requested to withdraw it on the assurance that the government will introduce a measure officially drafted to meet his case.

Between 1965 and 1969, two were brought forward in the Seanad, one (Protection of Animals (Amendment) Bill) became law in 1965 and the other was rejected on second stage.

PRIVATE BILLS

Private Bills are those promoted for the particular interest or benefit of any person or locality, as distinct from measures of public policy.

A Private Bill is, by virtue of the standing orders relating to private business, introduced in the Seanad after examination by the Examiner of Private Bills, (an officer appointed jointly by the Chairman of both Houses), to ensure compliance with standing orders regarding advertising, notification to people or bodies affected thereby and departments of state (see Chapter 10). After the second reading has been agreed to by the Seanad, the bill is referred to a joint committee of both Houses consisting of a chairman nominated by the Chairmen of both Houses, three deputies and three senators who have no personal, and in the case of deputies, whose constituents have no local interest in the bill.

The joint committee considers the bill, takes evidence, hears counsel on behalf of the promoters and objectors, considers reports from departments of state and reports the bill with or without amendments to both Houses.

Subsequently, the fourth and fifth stages are taken in the Seanad and the bill is sent to the Dáil where it is considered on fourth and

46

ifth stages only, the other three stages being waived. It is then enacted in the same way as a Public Bill.

Fees on scales set out in the standing orders relative to private business are payable by the promoters and opponents of Private Bills.

IO

COMMITTEES

No review of the functions of the Houses of the Oireachtas would be complete without reference to the committees set up by them and an outline of the work which they do.

Ireland's system of committees is based on the British model and contrasts with the complicated system to be found in the U.S.A. and France. In these countries, legislation is divided into distinct categories and each category is allocated to a standing committee. In the House of Representatives in the USA there are separate committees on ways and means, on appropriations, on the judiciary on foreign affairs, and in the Senate, committees on foreign relations and commerce. All proposed legislation is referred to the particular committee which has special cognisance of the subject on which is proposed to legislate. It reports the legislation with or without amendments, or adversely, or not at all to the parent House. The Committee on Finance in the Dáil resembles such committees but as has been pointed out (p. 38), it has a historical origin unconnected with the committee system as such. In the US system, a procedure analogous to that of the Committee on Finance is adopted to deal with money and ways and means (i.e. financial) resolutions.

Under the Irish system, a committee does not make final decisions It reports to the House which then decides. A special committee on a bill (corresponding to the standing committee in Britain) is a miniature of the committee of the whole House and is likely to judge the bill referred to it in the same way as the House would, thus relieving the House of the burden of committee work.

However, a select committee is normally set up to perform work for which the House is unsuited. Its type of investigation, which requires detailed inquiry, the examination of witnesses and the weighing of their evidence, is not one that a large assembly could conveniently perform. A bill reported from a select committee is recommitted to a committee of the whole House which has the advantage of having before it the report of the select committee containing its findings and opinions on the matters at issue, based on the expert advice to which it has had access.

At the commencement of every Dáil and Seanad, the Committee

f Selection and the Committees on Procedure and Privileges are ppointed.

ommittee of Selection: This committee consists of eleven members n the Dáil with a quorum of five, and eleven members, including he Leas-Chathaoirleach (Chairman *ex officio*), in the Seanad with . quorum of four. It nominates the members to serve on select or pecial committees, has power to discharge such members from ime to time for non-attendance or at their own request, and to ppoint others to replace those discharged. The Committee, in ommon with other committees of the Houses, is so constituted as o be impartially representative of the House. The number of nembers on this Committee and others which are provided for in he standing orders has been varied occasionally to ensure com-liance with the latter requirements.

ommittee on Procedure and Privileges: This Committee consists of ighteen members and the Ceann Comhairle (Chairman *ex officio*) vith a quorum of eight in the Dáil, and of ten members and the *athaoirleach (Chairman *ex officio*) and Leas-Chathaoirleach with quorum of five in the Seanad. It has power to consider matters of rocedure, to recommend any additions or amendments to the tanding orders and to consider and report on members' privileges.

The Dáil Committee may also consider any matter relating to the onditions or premises in which members carry out their duties vhich is not specifically referred to any other committee.

JOINT COMMITTEES

The following joint committees of both Houses are nominated y the Committees of Selection:

) *Joint Library Committee:* consisting usually of seven members f each House with two from each as quorum, assists and advises he Ceann Comhairle and the Cathaoirleach in the direction and ontrol of the Oireachtas Library.

ii) *Joint Restaurant Committee:* constituted in the same way as the library Committee, directs and controls the Oireachtas Restaurant.

iii) *Joint Committee on Standing Orders (Private Business):* consists f three members of each House and a Chairman nominated by the *eann Comhairle and Cathaoirleach jointly (this position tradi-ionally alternates between Leas-Cheann Comhairle and Leas-hathaoirleach), with a quorum of three (at least one from each

House). It nominates the members to serve on joint committees or private bills and can discharge and replace them.

It also considers reports from the Examiner of Private Bills that the standing orders have not been complied with by the promoters of these bills or as to the construction of standing orders and recommends whether they ought to be dispensed with and, if so, on what conditions.

(iv) *Joint Committee on Consolidation Bills:* consists of three members of each House, with two from each as quorum, and the minister responsible for the bill or his parliamentary secretary *ex officio*. The Committee considers Consolidation Bills referred to it. It has power to send for persons, papers and records, and reports the bill with or without amendments and its observations on it to both Houses.

SELECT COMMITTEES

Committee of Public Accounts: provides the last link in the chain of Dáil control over the finances of the state. It is appointed at the beginning of each financial year to examine and report to the Dáil upon the accounts which show the appropriation of the sums granted by the Dáil to meet public expenditure, and to suggest alterations and improvements in the form of the estimates submitted to the House. The annual report of the Comptroller and Auditor General containing his observations on the accounts, is referred to the Committee to facilitate its work.

The Comptroller and Auditor General is appointed by the President on the nomination of the Dáil (Article 33.2 of the Constitution). He controls all disbursements on behalf of the state and audits all accounts of moneys administered by or under the authority of the Oireachtas (Article 33.1). Pursuant to Article 33.4, he reports to the Dáil at stated periods determined by law (see Exchequer and Audit Departments Acts 1866 and 1921, as adapted by the Comptroller and Auditor General Act 1923, for particulars of duties and reports). Like a judge, he can be removed from office only for stated misbehaviour or incapacity, after resolutions have been passed by both Houses calling for his removal.

The Committee, which is nominated by the Committee of Selection, usually consists of twelve members, none of whom is a minister or parliamentary secretary, and has a quorum of four. Traditionally, the chairman is a member of the opposition. The committee has power to send for persons, papers and records.

The appropriation account for each vote sets out the amount expended and the amount granted, and is signed by the accounting officer (the secretary of the department or head of the office) responsible for the vote. It is accompanied by a certificate of the Comptroller and Auditor General stating that the account is correct. When necessary, notes from the accounting officer are appended to the account explaining substantial variations between the amounts granted and the amounts spent.

The Committee, in pursuance of its powers to send for persons, papers and records, examines the Comptroller and Auditor General, the accounting officers and officials of the Department of Finance, and their evidence is printed with the report of the Committee. Supplementary written information from witnesses required by the Committee is reproduced in appendices to the report.

The investigations of the Committee are made from a financial and not from a political point of view. It does not attempt any inquiry into matters of policy, which are determined by the Dáil: the amount of the estimates or the amount of any particular grant are matters of policy and it would be entirely outside the scope of the Committee to question these or to investigate the ground on which they are based.

The Committee of Public Accounts reports to the Dáil. In practice these reports are never debated but are administratively dealt with by the Department of Finance which indicates to the Committee by ministerial minute the steps it proposes to take to implement the Committee's recommendations, or, if it disagrees with them, the reasons why. In the next ensuing year, the Committee considers the finance minute on the report of the previous Committee and if disagreements cannot be resolved, the Dáil, as final arbiter, decides the issue.

It is settled practice that an excess vote arising from overexpenditure of an estimate and supplementary estimates, if there are any, may not be submitted to the Dáil without having been previously considered by the Committee. This is usually done at a meeting of the Committee convened specifically for the purpose and its recommendations form the subject of an interim report.*

Committee on Statutory Instruments: This is a committee of Seanad Éireann which examines instruments made by the government or

---

*See Epitome of the Reports from the Committee of Public Accounts on the Appropriation accounts from 1922–23 to 1933–34 and of the minutes of the Minister for Finance thereon, p. 88 et seq.

other bodies pursuant to statute and ensures that they comply with certain basic criteria set out in its terms of reference. The Seanad has equal powers with the Dáil to annul such orders. In fact, it may be argued that, in practice, the Upper House has superior powers, since the period of twenty-one sitting days during which an order is subject to annulment usually represents a considerably longer period in the life of the Seanad. Therefore, it was a natural development that this House would interest itself in the field of delegated legislation.

The Committee was first constituted as a sessional committee (i.e. for the life of the House) in 1948 and has been similarly reconstituted since then at the commencement of every Seanad.

Its original terms of reference have been modified in detail and the Committee, constituted in December 1969, was set up pursuant to the following resolution of the Seanad:

"(1) That a Select Committee, to be nominated by the Committee of Selection, be appointed to consider every Statutory Instrument laid, or laid in draft, before Seanad Éireann, in pursuance of a statutory requirement, with a view to determining whether the special attention of Seanad Éireann should be drawn to it on any of the following grounds:

(i)   that it imposes a charge on the public revenues or contains provisions requiring payments to be made to the Exchequer or any Government Department or to any local or public authority in consideration of any licence or consent, or of any services to be rendered, or prescribes the amount of any such charge or payments;

(ii) that it appears to make some unusual or unexpected use of the powers conferred by the Statute under which it is made;

(iii) that it purports to have retrospective effect where the parent Statute confers no express authority so to provide;

(iv) that there appears to have been unjustifiable delay either in the laying of it before Seanad Éireann or in its publication;

(v)   that for any special reason its form or purport calls for elucidation.

(2) That the Select Committee consist of nine members of whom three shall form a quorum.

(3) That the Select Committee have power to report from time to time and to require any Government Department or other

instrument-making authority concerned to submit a memorandum explaining any Statutory Instrument which may be under their consideration or to depute a representative to appear before them as a witness for the purpose of explaining any such Statutory Instrument.

(4) That it be the duty of the Committee before reporting that the special attention of Seanad Éireann should be drawn to any Statutory Instrument to afford to any Government Department or other instrument-making authority concerned therewith an opportunity of furnishing orally or in writing such explanations as the Department or authority may think fit, and the Select Committee have power to report to Seanad Éireann from time to time any memoranda submitted or other evidence given to them in explanation of any Statutory Instrument.

(5) That the explanatory memoranda submitted to the Select Committee appointed by Resolution of 7 July 1965 subsequent to its Report of 19 March 1969 be referred to the Committee for examination and report."

The final term of reference was incorporated to ensure the continuity of the work of the Select Committee. The Committee meets regularly and reports to the Seanad every twelve to eighteen months. Its reports draw the attention of the House to the instruments on the grounds set out in its terms of reference and also contain the minutes of evidence of witnesses summoned before the Committee and copies of the correspondence between the Committee and the departments or other instrument-making authorities.

II

SITTINGS AND BUSINESS OF THE HOUSES

The Constitution (Article 15.7) provides that the Houses shall hold at least one session every year. Article 15.8 states that the sittings of each House shall be public, but, in cases of special emergency, either House may hold a private sitting with the assent of two-thirds of the members present (no such private sitting has yet been held). The average sittings of the Houses between 1962 and 1971 were 82 days per year for the Dáil, and 29 days per year for the Seanad. The greater proportion of sitting days in each House is in the period preceding the summer recess which generally occurs about the end of July or the beginning of August.

DÁIL ÉIREANN

Under standing orders, the Dáil, unless it otherwise resolves, meets every Tuesday and Wednesday at 3 p.m. and every Thursday at 10.30 a.m., and adjourns not later than 11 p.m. on Tuesdays and Wednesdays and not later than 5.30 p.m. on Thursdays. However, the days and hours may be varied or extended, depending on the state of business in the House.

Every sitting of the Dáil is governed by a printed Order Paper which is prepared under the direction of the Ceann Comhairle. The Taoiseach has the right to determine the order in which government business shall appear on the Order Paper and he announces at the commencement of public business the order in which it is to be taken each day.

On Tuesdays and Wednesdays, questions are answered normally at 3 p.m. On Thursdays, questions are taken at 2.30 p.m. Second comes private business which relates to private bills and ancillary matters (to be distinguished from Private Members' Bills which are public bills introduced by private members). Then the House proceeds to deal with public business, including motions relating to the introduction of bills and orders of the day, i.e. business previously ordered by the House to be set down for that day.

On Tuesdays and Wednesdays, unless the House otherwise orders, private members' business is taken from 6 p.m. to 7.30 p.m.

The following table indicates the principal business transacted by the Dáil in the period 1963–1971 and the time devoted to financial business (estimates, budget debates and proposals for legislation consequential on them) and private members' motions.

TABLE III.

Year	Number of sittings of Dáil	Total number of hours of sitting	Parliamentary questions		Financial business	Private members' business
			oral	written		
	(no.)	(hours)	(no.)	(no.)	(hours)	(hours)
1963	86	606	4,106	316	295	27
1964	70	510	3,427	271	245	16½
1965	66	471	4,011	207	233	10
1966	93	708	4,328	308	349	36
1967	78	570	3,733	246	279	16½
1968	81	582	4,717	214	220	30
1969	78	569	5,139	331	207	15
1970	89	712	5,270	291	286	1½
1971	99	835	6,056	499	366	27

Government time to debate private members' motions was allocated as follows:

1963 – 12½ hours (involving 2 motions)
1971 – 7½ hours (involving 3 motions)

SEANAD ÉIREANN

Under its standing orders, the Seanad, unless it otherwise resolves, meets on Wednesdays and Thursdays at 3 p.m. and on Fridays at 10.30 a.m. The sittings, however, are largely dependent on the volume of business sent to the House from the Dáil. While the Dáil is discussing the estimates, very little legislation is passed by it and the Seanad has no occasion to meet. The disparity in sittings between the two Houses is explained first by the difference in the number of members of each and, secondly, by the fact that debates similar to those in the Dáil on the Budget and the estimates do not take place in the Seanad.

Every sitting is governed by an Order Paper which is prepared under the direction of the Cathaoirleach. Government bills take precedence over all other business except private business.

The order of precedence of government bills, which form the greatest proportion of the work of the Seanad, is decided by the Leader of the House after consultation with other interested parties. (The Leader of the House is a member of the House who supports the government and who moves motions for resolutions and bills on behalf of the government; non-members of the House, such as members of the government and parliamentary secretaries, may not move motions in the House). However, under standing orders, bills coming from the Dáil, other than money bills, and bills the time for the consideration of which by the Seanad shall have been abridged (Article 24 of the Constitution), cannot be considered before the expiration of three clear days after receipt from the Dáil, unless the Seanad otherwise orders.

The following table sets out the number and total hours of sittings of the Seanad in the period 1963-1971. Approximately 90-95 per cent. of the work consisted of the consideration of legislation sent to the second chamber by the Dáil.

TABLE IV.

Year	Number of sittings of Seanad	Total number of hours of sittings
1963	27	139
1964	17	106
1965	29	227
1966	37	239
1967	35	210
1968	33	236
1969	22	136
1970	29	198
1971	47	332

12

POWERS AND THE DUTIES OF CHAIRMEN OF THE HOUSES

Article 15.9.1° of the Constitution provides that each House shall elect from its members its own Chairman and Deputy Chairman and shall prescribe their powers and duties.

CHAIRMAN OF DÁIL (CEANN COMHAIRLE)

The standing orders of the Dáil devolve duties and confer authority upon the Chairman in matters concerning the conduct of proceedings and the general business and administration of the House.

The Chairman presides over the sittings of the Dáil and while doing so he is the sole judge of order. He calls on members to speak and all speeches must be addressed to him. He puts all questions that have to be put to the House, supervises divisions and declares the results of these. He has the authority to suppress disorder during the sitting and to enforce prompt obedience to his ruling, and he may order members to withdraw from the House or name them for suspension by the House for a specified period. He may adjourn the House if the proceedings become too disorderly. The Chairman has a wide variety of duties to do with the general business of the Dáil. The Order Paper which governs each sitting of the House is prepared under his direction. Each parliamentary question, motion or amendment which is tabled by a member is examined by him to ensure that it complies with the standing orders and precedents, and where it does not do so, he may disallow it or, after consultation with the member, amend it. It is within his discretion to accept questions, motions or amendments on shorter notice than that provided for in the standing orders and to accept during the course of a sitting certain formal motions relating to the sitting or its business.

The Chairman is in control of and responsible for the administration (secretariat) of the Dáil. The minutes of proceedings of the House are perused and signed by him; when printed, these constitute the Journal of the Proceedings. The official Report of Debates is issued under his supervision. Under him and subject to his orders, the Clerk of the House has direction and control over all the officers and clerks.

The Chairman is *ex officio* Chairman of the Committee on Procedure and Privileges of the Dáil.

Since the Chairman cannot physically preside over every sitting of the Dáil, the Deputy Chairman, when deputising, exercises the powers of the Chairman. However, the standing order relating to closure of debates can be put in force only when the Chairman is in the Chair; it is the practice for the Deputy Chairman to send for the Chairman when a member has been suspended.

The Constitution confers the following powers and functions on the Chairman of the Dáil:

membership of the Commission which exercises the powers and performs the functions of the President in his absence or incapacity (Article 14.2.1°)

ex officio membership of the Council of State which aids and counsels the President in the exercise and performance of certain of his powers and functions (Article 31.2)

certification of bills which, in his opinion, are money bills (Article 22.2)

possession and exercise of a casting vote in the event of an equality of votes in the Dáil (Article 15.11.2°).

The office of the Chairman of the Dáil, as prescribed in the standing orders and under the Constitution, is characterised by its authority and impartiality. He represents the House in all its external relations. He takes no part in political activity or in debate. His rulings are respected by all sides of the House, may not be criticised by any member except on a formal motion, and are regarded as precedents to be followed by subsequent Chairmen.

CHAIRMAN OF SEANAD (CATHAOIRLEACH)

The standing orders of the Seanad devolve duties and confer authority upon the Chairman in matters concerning the conduct of proceedings and the general business and administration of the House. These duties and powers do not differ significantly from those conferred on the Chairman of the Dáil.

The Constitution confers the following powers and functions on the Chairman of the Seanad:

membership of the Commission which exercises the powers and performs the functions of the President in his absence and incapacity (Article 14.2.1°)

ex officio membership of the Council of State which aids and

counsels the President in implementing certain powers and functions
(Article 31.2)
possession and exercise of a casting vote in the event of an equality
of votes in the Seanad (Article 15.11.2°).

DEBATES AND JOURNALS

Debates

An official report of the debates of each House in oratio recta is
published under the supervision of the Chairman. Daily unrevised
reports are published initially within two or three days of the sittings
to which they refer. They are periodically revised, collated, indexed,
bound and published in volumes. A debate is referred to by giving
the number of the volume and the relevant columns.

Journals

Journals of proceedings of the Houses contain daily records of
the res gestae of the Houses compiled from the minutes made by the
Clerks. They constitute the permanent official record and are
accepted in all courts as prima facie evidence of what has been done
in the Houses (section 2 of the Documentary Evidence Act 1925).
A copy of each journal (or imeachta) is initialled and signed by the
Chairman of the House. In common with all other records and
documents belonging to the Houses, the journals are retained in the
custody of the Clerks and may not be removed without the express
permission of the House concerned (or by the Chairman of the
House, if the House is adjourned for any period longer than a week).
The journals are published daily and are subsequently indexed and
published annually in bound form.

13

ADMINISTRATION

Dáil Eireann and Seanad Éireann are assisted by a secretariat which is referred to as the Office of the Houses of the Oireachtas. The standing orders of the Dáil provide for the offices of Clerk and Clerk-Assistant of the Dáil, and the standing orders of the Seanad provide for the offices of Clerk and Clerk-Assistant of the Seanad.

The Clerk of the Dáil (and in his absence the Clerk-Assistant) has direction and control over all the officers and clerks in the House, subject to such orders as he may receive from the Chairman of the Dáil. The Clerk of the Seanad (and in his absence the Clerk-Assistant) has direction and control over the same staff subject to such orders as he may receive from the Chairman of the Seanad.

The appointment of the Clerk and Clerk-Assistant of the Dáil is made by the Taoiseach on the joint recommendation of the Chairman of the Dáil and the Minister for Finance, and the appointment of the Clerk and Clerk-Assistant of the Seanad is made by the Taoiseach on the joint recommendation of the Chairman of the Seanad and the Minister for Finance (sections 5 and 6 of the Staff of the Houses of the Oireachtas Act 1959).

The functions of the Office of the Houses of the Oireachtas include the preparation of the Order Paper and the Journal of Proceedings of each House, the issue of an Official Report of the Debates of each House, the custody of all records and other documents belonging to the Houses, and administrative, clerical and subordinate work associated with the sittings and business of the Houses and of its committees.

Appendix I

SEANAD ELECTORAL (PANEL MEMBERS) ACTS 1947 AND 1954

Register of Nominating Bodies entitled to nominate persons to the panels of candidates for the purpose of every Seanad general election, revised at the annual revision and signed by the Seanad Returning Officer in pursuance of section 19 of the Seanad Electoral (Panel Members) Act 1947, as amended by the Seanad Electoral (Panel Members) Act 1954 (as revised on 16 March, 1973).

Cultural and Educational Panel

Royal Irish Academy	19 Dawson Street, Dublin 2
Cumann Leabharlann na hÉireann (The Library Association of Ireland)	46 Grafton Street, Dublin 2
Irish National Teachers' Organisation	35 Parnell Square, Dublin 1
Association of Secondary Teachers, Ireland	11 Hume Street, Dublin 2
An Cumann Ghairm-Oideachais i n-Éireann (The Irish Vocational Education Association)	Central Technical Institute, Waterford
The Incorporated Law Society of Ireland	Solicitors' Buildings, Four Courts, Dublin 7
Cumann Dochtúirí na hÉireann (The Irish Medical Association)	10 Fitzwilliam Place, Dublin 2
Royal College of Surgeons in Ireland	123 St. Stephen's Green, Dublin 2
Dental Board	57 Merrion Square, Dublin 2
Veterinary Council	53 Lansdowne Road, Ballsbridge, Dublin 4
The Pharmaceutical Society of Ireland	18 Shrewsbury Road, Ballsbridge, Dublin 4
The General Council of the Bar of Ireland	Law Librar. Four Courts, Dublin 7
Bantracht na Tuaithe (Irish Country-women's Association)	5 Merrion Road, Ballsbridge, Dublin 4
Royal Society of Antiquaries of Ireland	63 Merrion Square, Dublin 2
Muintir na Gaeltachta	51 Sráid Móintseó, Baile Átha Cliath 7
The Royal Irish Academy of Music	36/38 Westland Row, Dublin 2
Irish Dental Association	29 Kenilworth Square, Dublin 6
The Irish Georgian Society	Castletown House, Celbridge, Co. Kildare
Cumann le Seandacht Átha Cliath (The Old Dublin Society)	City Assembly House, 58 Sth. William Street, Dublin 2

Agricultural Panel

Royal Dublin Society	Post Office Box No. 121, Ballsbridge, Dublin 4

61

6

The Irish Agricultural Organisation Society Limited	The Plunkett House, 84 Merrion Square, Dublin 2
National Executive of the Irish Live Stock Trade	627 North Circular Road, Dublin 1
The Irish Bloodstock Breeders' Association	9 Merrion Square, Dublin 2
The Sugar Beet and Vegetable Section Limited, Irish Farmers' Association	The Irish Farm Centre, Naas Road, Bluebell, Dublin 12
The Irish Creamery Managers' Association	33 Kildare Street, Dublin 2
Munster Agricultural Society	21 Cook Street, Cork
The Council of Boards of Fishery Conservators	"Kendale", Ballincar, Sligo
General Council of Committees of Agriculture	County Offices, Friary Road, Naas, Co. Kildare

Labour Panel

Irish Congress of Trade Unions	Congress House, 19 Raglan Road, Dublin 4
The Irish Conference of Professional and Service Associations	4 North Great George's Street, Dublin 1

Industrial and Commercial Panel

Association of Chambers of Commerce of Ireland	7 Clare Street, Dublin 2
The Confederation of Irish Industry	28 Fitzwilliam Place, Dublin 2
The Construction Industry Federation	9 Leeson Park, Dublin 6
The Society of the Irish Motor Industry	5 Upper Pembroke Street, Dublin 2
Licensed Vintners' Association	L.V.A. Centre, Anglesea Road, Ballsbridge, Dublin 4
RGDATA—The Irish Retail Grocers' Association	24 Earlsfort Terrace, Dublin 2
Irish Auctioneers' and Valuers' Institute	38 Merrion Square East, Dublin 2
Irish Banks' Standing Committee	91 Pembroke Road, Ballsbridge, Dublin 4
The Insurance Institute of Ireland	32 Nassau Street, Dublin 2
The Institute of Chartered Accountants in Ireland	7 Fitzwilliam Place, Dublin 2
The Royal Institute of the Architects of Ireland	8 Merrion Square, Dublin 2
The Federated Union of Employers	8 Fitzwilliam Place, Dublin 2
The Irish Hotels Federation	13 Northbrook Road, Dublin 6
The Association of Advertisers in Ireland Limited	44 Lower Leeson Street, Dublin 2
The Irish National Vintners' Federation Limited	134 St. Stephen's Green West, Dublin 2

The Institute of Advertising Practitioners in Ireland	35 Upper Fitzwilliam Street, Dublin 2
The Licensed Road Transport Association	58 Burrin Street, Carlow
National Development Association (Forbairt)	Ireland House, St. Stephen's Green North, Dublin 2
Road Transport Organisation	The Transport Centre, 34 Upper O'Connell Street, Dublin 1
The National Wholesale Confectioners' Association	27 South Frederick Street, Dublin 2
The Institution of Engineers of Ireland	22 Clyde Road, Ballsbridge, Dublin 4
The Institute of Certified Public Accountants in Ireland	20 Earlsfort Terrace, Dublin 2

Administrative Panel

Irish County Councils General Council	1–2 Cavendish Row, Dublin 1
The Association of Municipal Authorities of Ireland	Town Hall, Mallow, Co. Cork
Central Remedial Clinic	Vernon Avenue, Clontarf, Dublin 3
The National Association for Cerebral Palsy (Ireland) Limited	St. Brendan's, Sandymount Avenue, Ballsbridge, Dublin 4

Appendix II

RECOMMENDATIONS OF THE JOINT COMMITTEE ON THE ELECTORAL LAW IN RELATION TO ELIGIBILITY FOR ELECTION

(a) *Legal Disqualifications:* The Joint Committee (paragraphs 100–103 of its Final Report T.184 dated 12 July, 1961) disagreed with the proposal to retain the existing legal disqualifications. It stated:—

"The proposal is to continue the existing disqualifications with modifications which would make them more readily workable. The Joint Committee does not feel that a good case exists for the continuance of these disqualifications. The Committee feels that electors must be regarded as mature enough to elect representatives of the type they want and to take the consequences of their choice should the persons elected become incapable of acting during their period of office by reason of imprisonment, mental instability or bankruptcy. It is noteworthy that this principle applies to the office of President, for which there are no statutory disqualifications. The Committee feels, however, that an exception should be made in the case of a person convicted of treason, as defined in Article 39 of the Constitution, or of an offence under the Official Secrets Acts. Such a person should be disqualified for membership, if he is a member, but he should not be disqualified for standing at the consequential bye-election or any subsequent election.

On individual disqualifications, the Joint Committee feels that the fact that a person, in addition to suffering the normal penalties of imprisonment and/or a fine, will, if he is a member of the Dáil or Seanad be disqualified for membership if a sentence of penal servitude or imprisonment exceeding six months—or any other period specified—is imposed, make a court hesitate to impose a sentence exceeding the specified period, even if it considers such a sentence justified. Thus the disqualification on account of a sentence of imprisonment may have the effect of mitigating the penalties instead of being an additional penalty as intended.

The trend in recent legislation has been to do away with the distinction between physical and mental ill-health. A member suffering from a disease which prevents him for a long time from discharging his functions as a public representative is not thereby disqualified. The Joint Committee does not see any logic in this distinction.

The abolition of the disqualification on account of bankruptcy would follow from the acceptance of the principle of full electoral responsibility, in accordance with which the Joint Committee recommends the abolition of the other disqualifications."

The Joint Committee also recommended the repeal of the specific disqualifications for membership of the Dáil and Seanad on account of corrupt and illegal practices. It may be noted that, in accordance with an analogous recommendation of the Joint Committee (paragraph 90 of the Final Report), the Electoral Act 1963 repealed the disenfranchisement provisions following a conviction for corrupt and illegal practices, treason or felony, which had been a feature of the law until then.

The Joint Committee also recommended the proposal to repeal the provisions of the Central Bank Act 1942, which imposed a disqualification for membership of the Houses of the Oireachtas on the Governor and directors of the Central Bank. All recent legislation relating to semi-state bodies declares that a member of the Dáil or Seanad may not be a member of a state-sponsored body and that if any member of the body becomes a member of the Dáil or Seanad he must cease to be a member of the body. The principle followed in these cases is that the Oireachtas has the prior claim to the person's services, and membership of the Oireachtas is incompatible with membership of the semi-state body.

(b) *Legal Incapacities:* The departmental proposal relating to incapacities for membership of both Houses was as follows:

(1) A person shall be incapable of being elected or being a member of either House of the Oireachtas, who is

   (a) a wholetime member of the Defence Forces

   (b) a member of the Garda Síochána

   (c) a civil servant

   (d) a district justice

   (e) a lay member of the Irish Land Commission, or

   (f) an "officer of the Houses of the Oireachtas" as defined in the Civil Service Regulation Act 1956, as amended by the Staff of the Houses of the Oireachtas Act 1959.

64

A wholetime member of the Defence Forces is defined as follows:

(i) A member of the Permanent Defence Force, or

(ii) an officer of the Reserve Defence Force employed continuously on military service or duty during a period which a proclamation authorising the calling out of reservists on permanent service is in force, or during a period during which reservists are called out on permanent service under section 88 of the Defence Act 1954, or

(iii) a reservist called out on permanent service.

A civil servant is defined as a person who is a civil servant for the purposes of the Civil Service Regulation Act 1956, as amended.

(2) Where a member of either House of the Oireachtas becomes incapable of being a member of either House, whether by virtue of this section or by reason of his appointment as judge or Comptroller and Auditor General, he shall be deemed to have resigned his seat and shall notify the Chairman of the House as soon as possible. The Chairman shall report accordingly to the House as soon as practicable. Where a member of either House of the Oireachtas becomes a member of the Reserve Defence Force (who is not a wholetime member of the Defence Forces), he shall be deemed to have resigned his seat and shall notify the Chairman of the House, as soon as possible, and the latter shall report accordingly to the House as soon as practicable.

(3) Provide for a penalty for failure to notify the Chairman under the provisions of this proposal.

The Final Report (paragraphs 106 to 111) of the Joint Committee states, *inter alia:*

"The Joint Committee agrees . . . that a civil servant should do nothing to give colour to any suggestion that his official actions are in any way influenced or capable of being influenced by party motives. This is of vital importance for civil servants concerned with the formulation of policy or employed in any clerical or supervisory position and it is undesirable that such persons should be permitted to stand for election.

The same considerations do not apply with such force to persons in other grades in the civil service. In this connexion the Joint Committee had before it representations which adverted to the freedom allowed to various grades of civil servants in the United Kingdom to engage in political activities. The Committee also considered section 9 of the Electricity (Supply) (Amendment) Act 1958, under which an officer or servant of the Electricity Supply Board who becomes a member of either House of the Oireachtas may be seconded from his employment with the Board for the period of his membership. The tendency in recent legislation is to allow a similar freedom to employees of other state bodies. This tendency accords with the principle suggested in the note to the first proposal in Part IV of this Report that the Legislature should have first claim on a person's services. The Committee is in full agreement with this principle. It is of the utmost importance that the Legislature should be able to draw for its members from as wide a field as possible, and only for the gravest and most compelling reasons of public policy should any individual be prevented from putting himself forward for election. The Committee, having considered the question with great care, is of opinion that such reasons do not exist in the case of persons employed in the manipulative grades in the Department of Posts and Telegraphs and corresponding grades in other Departments, and that the existence of the existing prohibition gives rise to indefensible anomalies as between workers in the Electricity Supply Board and other Boards or authorities financed wholly or largely by the State who can stand for election without penalty, while those in, say, the Department of Posts and Telegraphs cannot stand without losing their positions. The Committee, accordingly, recommends that civil servants in manipulative grades in the Department of Posts and Telegraphs and corresponding grades in other Departments should be permitted to stand for election to the Dáil or Seanad on the same conditions as apply in the case of an employee of the Electricity Supply Board.

Under sections 48 and 74 of the Defence Act 1954, a member of the Reserve Defence Force must, on becoming a member of either House of the Oireachtas, cease to be a member of the Reserve. Membership of either House of the Oireachtas, which requires attendance at Dublin, may conflict with membership of the Reserve Defence Force which may require attendance elsewhere. It is, however, reasonable to assume that the times at which this conflict will arise will be limited and it is not in the best interests of the State to deprive a member of the Reserve Defence Force of his position in the Force because he becomes a member of the Dáil or Seanad. The Joint Committee considers the converse to be true also—that a member of the Dáil or Seanad who joins or is in the Reserve should not on that account cease to be a member.

If, however, reservists are called out on permanent service, the conflict would arise in an acute form. In such a case, the Joint Committee recommends that a reservist who is a member of either House should at his option be given leave from the Defence Forces while his membership of the House continues. If he does not avail himself of this leave, then his membership of the House should cease. The Committee appreciates that this recommendation seems to imply that when a reservist is most needed, that is, when he is called out on permanent service, he need not go. The Committee, however, considers that the principle that the Legislature has the prior claim on a person's service is sufficient justification of its proposal in the matter. It recommends the provisions of this proposal in regard to the Defence Forces subject to these modifications.

Where a member of either House becomes incapable by reason of his appointment to a post entailing incapacity for membership, it is proposed to place an obligation on him to notify the Chairman of the House of his incapacity and to provide penalties for failure to do so. The Joint Committee recommends that this obligation should be placed instead on the authority which appoints him to the post and that no provision should be made for penalties for failure to notify incapacity.

Subject to the reservations in the preceding paragraphs, the Joint Committee recommends these proposals."

Appendix III

INFORMAL COMMITTEE ON REFORM OF DÁIL PROCEDURE

SUMMARY OF RECOMMENDATIONS

(a) *Questions to Ministers.*
  (1) Question time to be variable by Order of the House, and practice of carrying over unanswered Questions to be regularised.

(2) Member not present to receive written reply unless Question postponed before 5 p.m. on previous day.

(3) Order of Ministers answering to rotate when Questions carried over. No Questions to Taoiseach on Thursdays.

(4) Members to be asked to agree to informal requests for postponements of Questions if notice found inadequate.

(5) Questions seeking statistical information only, to be starred for written reply.

(6) Position of Ceann Comhairle in regard to replies incorporated in Official Report to be clarified.

(b) *Adjournment Debates* (*Urgent Public Importance*).

(7) New criteria to be adopted for adjournment debates on urgent matters.

(c) *Government Bills.*

(8) Provision to be made for presentation, printing and circulation of Government Bills before First Stage taken in House.

(9) When motion for leave to introduce Bill is opposed, statements not to exceed five minutes.

(10) When question disposing of amendment to motion for Second Reading of Bill is carried, Bill to be deemed to be read a second time without further question being put.

(11) Money Resolutions to be abolished. Messages of Recommendation to be received before Committee Stage and to be printed on Order Paper.

(12) Financial Resolutions incidental to Bills to be taken only in the House.

(13) Provision to be made in Standing Orders confirming present practice of prohibiting private members moving amendments to Bill which could have the effect of imposing or increasing charges on the revenue or on the people.

(14) More Committee Stages to be taken in Special Committees.

(15) Parties to be empowered to nominate substitutes to replace and vote instead of absent Members of Special Committee.

(16) Bills reported from Special Committee to be taken in the House on Report without first being recommitted to a Committee of the whole Dáil.

(17) Public and Press to be admitted to Special and other Committees normally.

(18) Proceedings on Fourth Stage to be confined to dealing with amendments if any.

(d) *Financial Business.*

(19) Estimates and Budget Resolutions to be taken only in the House.

(20) Standing Order 121 (presentation of Estimates) to be amended to meet any change in the financial year.

(21) Time limits to be imposed on speeches in debates on Estimates and Financial Resolutions.

(22) Motions to refer back or reduce Estimates to be abolished and proposing of amendments to Estimates not to be allowed.

(e) *Private Members' Business.*

(23) Private Members' business to be eligible to be taken throughout the year; the Government to have the right to appropriate the time for a specified period on any day without notice.

(24) Party or Parties in Government, while entitled to participate in arrangements for nominating business, to be discouraged from doing so when time is limited.

(25) Bills to enjoy no priority over Motions in order of business, except when selected by group exercising its right in rotation.

(26) Private Member to be allowed to initiate Bill without leave of House if nominated by group and if no other Bill sponsored by group before the House.

(27) Time limit of six hours to apply to second reading debates on private Members' Bills and same time limits on speeches to apply as in case of Motions.

(28) Private Member to be prohibited from introducing Bill main object of which is imposition of charge.

(f) *Sittings.*

(29) Dáil to sit on Church Holiday falling on prescribed sitting day.

(g) *Divisions.*

(30) Number of Members entitled to demand division to be raised from five to ten.

(31) Arrangements for taking divisions on Estimate Motions at 10.15 p.m. to be made permanent.

(h) *Debate.*

(32) Reopening of discussion on matter discussed within preceding six months to be prohibited.

(33) Chair to be empowered to order Member to discontinue his speech if he is irrelevant, is repetitious or speaks for purpose of obstructing business.

(34) Requirement that motions and amendments be seconded to be dropped.

i) *Technical Amendments of Standing Orders.*
(35) Amendments to Standing Orders of a drafting or technical nature to be made as recommended by Ceann Comhairle.